SEEING EYE HUMAN

SEEING EYE HUMAN

how an overprotective dog came to need protection

JENNIFER A. CARLE

Tate Publishing & *Enterprises*

Seeing Eye Human

This title is also available as a Tate Out Loud product. Visit www.tatepublishing.com for more information.

Published by Tate Publishing & Enterprises, LLC
127 E. Trade Center Terrace | Mustang, Oklahoma 73064 USA
1.888.361.9473 | www.tatepublishing.com

Tate Publishing is committed to excellence in the publishing industry. The company reflects the philosophy established by the founders, based on Psalms 68:11,
"The Lord gave the word and great was the company of those who published it."

Cover design by Steven Jeffrey
Interior design by Janae J. Glass

Published in the United States of America

ISBN: 978-1-60462-233-1
1. Pets: Dogs: General 2. Family & Relationships

07.10.02

I would like to thank my wonderful and supportive family who never complained when I left the room to "write down this little thought." I would also like to extend my deepest appreciation for those people, young and old, who continue to come to our house despite being growled and barked at.

This book would not be possible without Winn. Winn would not be possible without the caring and compassionate employees and volunteers at the Maryland SPCA, and without the patient guidance of trainer extraordinaire Janet Boss and Best Friends Dog Obedience.

A special thank you must also go to the loving and nurturing doctors and staff of Main Street Veterinary Hospital, Vet Dermatologists, and the Veterinary Ophthalmology Clinic. You have made Winn's last years and months with us very comfortable and happy.

This book is also dedicated to all the people out there who realize a dog is not just a pet, but a true member of the family.

PREFACE

I don't know when it was, exactly, that my dog, Winn, became blind. She had no night vision in her left eye during the middle part of her thirteenth year. She'd fall off the curb at night when it was dark and look around her with an expression of embarrassment on her face. I would reassure her that nobody saw. She would wag her tail and continue on our walk sniffing out the newest aromas.

In April of 2006, Winn became disoriented. She was panting and pacing and seemed agitated. After hours of trying to determine whether she needed to go out or sleep in a different room, I took her to the all-night animal clinic thinking she needed to be euthanized. The staff was wonderful at the hospital. They gave me a box of tissues and patiently waited as I hiccupped through my sobs that I thought she had suffered a stroke. The veterinarian gave Winn a full physical and diagnosed the problem as the onset of dementia. We left with a prescription for anxiety (hers, not mine although I probably could have used a pill as well), and came home and waited for her sleep to come. Winn fell asleep at 6:00 a.m., the time that the rest of the house is waking.

As I sat on Winn's bed stroking her soft fur, waiting for sleep to descend upon her, I remembered back to the day I decided I needed a dog to fulfill the void in my life.

WINSOME

In 1991 I moved from my sheltered life in Baltimore City to the unknown and unfamiliar. I took up residence in a surfing town in southern California. Considering I am not one to take uncalculated risks, I left with the stipulation that I would return to the Baltimore area in one year, move back to my home that I was renting out for that year, and resume my position as a behavioral specialist working with the developmentally disabled. I moved into a tiny apartment with a guy I knew from my high school days.

I had saved enough money so I wouldn't need to work for several months in order to find "the right job." I didn't want to sell myself out and waste my education by working just anywhere. My first few days were spent relaxing by the pool with copies of various fashion magazines. After about a week of this, I decided I needed more of a mental challenge and began bringing the *L.A. Times* poolside. I meant to use my pen to circle ads for the perfect job. I, instead, tucked into the daily crossword puzzles. One of the definitions stumped me. It asked for a seven letter word meaning "child-like charm." I had no idea what this word could be and spent the rest of the afternoon laying in my lounge chair working the other clues in order to figure out this answer. By the end of the day, it came to me—winsome. To have child-like charm or cheeriness is to be winsome. I had never heard the word before, but I was determined to make it my own. I was going to become winsome!

A few days later I was not only winsome, I was bored. I took the first job that hired me and pretended I was leading an enviable life in California away from the family and provinciality in Baltimore that I suddenly and desperately missed.

I worked at a dating service until I was fired for turning down the advances of the owner. Apparently having a boyfriend was not a good enough reason to reject him.

My year in California turned into two; certainly not for my love of the place. I couldn't stand the lack of depth of the people around me. I missed Baltimore. I missed my friends who promised to visit but never did. I missed the gossip, being the subject of gossip. I'd hit a new low. My boyfriend did not agree with my perception of the state he thought was so wonderful. He had told me that he loved me, but then when I told him of my plans to move back home, he told me he didn't love me anymore. He wasn't even sure he really ever had. I was not surprised. It seemed like the typical ambivalent attitude I had come to know. As I packed my bags, bike and clothes to wear to my job interview in Baltimore the following week, I realized that I was not winsome and probably never would be. I was too adult and too cynical to go back to the carefree days of my childhood. Was I carefree? Looking back, I could not ever imagine being so.

I settled into my new job, returned to my old house and tried to recapture all that I lost during the past two years. A couple of weekends spent with my friends at the local bar was all it took to realize that, with the exception of a new shopping complex in Towson, nothing else had changed. It was good to be home again.

WIN SOME; LOSE SOME

I threw myself into my new job as the manager of the petite department of a local department store. Having worked for two years with people who did not have the strong work ethic that I was brought up with, I looked forward to being with people who enjoyed coming to work, moving displays around and selling our fabulous merchandise. I came to work early and stayed late rearranging the jeans on the display counter, refolding sweaters, and cleaning out dressing rooms. I knew I needed to delegate these responsibilities, but this was my department, and I wanted to show pride of ownership.

A friend of mine came to visit me at work one day. While I was too busy to have lunch, I did agree to have a cup of coffee with her. She gently suggested that my work might be counterproductive. She mentioned the fact that I was not dating anyone, and she seemed to recognize a correlation between my need to refold already perfectly folded sweaters and my desire to stay away from my adorable, yet lonely, house. Being the true friend that she was (and still is), she wanted to introduce me to someone she worked for. I tried to tell her that I didn't have the time, but she had already given him my number and told me to expect a call.

The phone did ring, but it was not from the mystery date, it was from my former flame in California. He decided to move back to Baltimore to be closer to his aging parents. He wanted to resume our relationship, and he wanted to move in with me as soon as he got into town. I told him we'd need to talk more in depth when he arrived. I didn't want someone who loved me then didn't and maybe never had squishing my heart again.

He came back into town with a new perspective on our relationship and decided that he really did love me, he was just so hurt by my decision to move back home from California that he just "said" he didn't love me. In fact, he loved me even more than he ever had, and couldn't wait to resume our relationship. I was skeptical to say the very least, but I called my friend and told her not to have her employer call me for a date. She was mortified at my decision to begin anew with this guy who proved to be so unreliable so many times. She said that she would check back with me to two weeks.

So, I put my energies into making this relationship work for both of us. It started with a lease. My guy was going to pay half of everything, just like we had in California—right down to the groceries. He was stunned by my lack of trust in him and his desire to make a go of his newfound love for me. He signed the lease and moved into the spare bedroom. He began a job with regular 9–5 hours. I stayed in retail and continued working very irregular hours. During the Christmas season, I never came home before midnight. He was sure I was seeing someone else.

By February, I realized our long floundering relationship was just about out of steam. We went to Connecticut to visit my best friend from college and her boyfriend. They had been dating for years and were, in my mind, the perfect couple. They were beautiful in their looks and in their actions. They cared so deeply for one another. My heart ached for that. On the drive home, I told my guy that I wanted him to either marry me or break up with me. The rest of the four hour drive was silent. I hoped by the time we got back home he would give me his answer. He didn't. He told me that he didn't want to marry me, but he didn't want to break up with me either. I told him he needed to choose soon and give me an answer in week.

I felt exhilarated! No matter what the outcome of the decision was, my life was going to change significantly. This was huge! I had never done anything without planning it to the letter. I was letting someone else choose my fate, and *I was okay with it!* My heart was light, and I felt like I would take flight at any moment. I was free! I was *winsome!*

At the end of the week he did choose to break up with me, and I was ecstatic! I bought my favorite flower—tulips—and put them in vases all over the house. I rearranged my closets. I planned dinner parties. I quit my job in retail. I welcomed and embraced the new me.

I read the paper with renewed interest. I had my trusty pen in hand and began circling carefully. Not for a job this time, but for a dog.

I'VE GOT THE NAME, NOW I NEED THE DOG

I decided to go to the Maryland SPCA instead of a breeder. I wanted to rescue a dog. It seemed like the right thing to do. I visited the SPCA on April 5, 1994. I went in with an open mind that I may not find *the one*. I looked in the rows and rows of cages at the various sizes, colors, personalities and breed combinations. There were so many dogs. It was heartbreaking to me that people could just discard their pet like yesterday's newspaper. Who could give up such love? I thought I would be sick. I wanted them all from a moral stand point. I had lots of love to share. Come live with me! All of you!

I went back to the adoption counter where a counselor told me that the dogs and all of the animals, for that matter, were very well taken care of and that they kept all of the animals for as long as they could until someone adopted them.

She told me that it was okay to come back on another day and look again. My dog, *the one*, might come to the shelter some other time. I could come back as often as I wanted and take my time. The SPCA would never want any of their animals to go to a home that didn't work for all parties involved. I was so reassured by her kindness, though heartbroken still at the thought that the parade of animals coming to the shelter never ends.

I took one last trip through the kennels. There were a couple of dogs that were possibilities. One dog, a husky mix, was definitely worth giving a second look, but I noticed the information card was missing from his cage. This meant that someone was interested in him and an adoption was in the works if the human interview proved successful. I took my time and noticed that several of the dog cages had missing information cards. Many of these dogs had potential homes! The burden of my earlier sadness at the thought of dogs and other animals being discarded lifted. I walked back up the aisle and looked at the dogs on the other side. There she was. *The one.*

Her information card told me that she was a female lab mix. She was found on the side of the road in Baltimore City. She had been with the SPCA for three weeks, and she may have been house broken. She was rescued with no collar or tags, so the folks at the SPCA had named her Misty. Oh, she was the sweetest girl in the world! Her eyes were the most beautiful and insightful shade of brown. Her coat was black and so shiny. The SPCA had taken such wonderful care of her. She sat way in the back of her cage. She was very shy. When I squatted down on my knees to get a closer look, she ducked her head down, but she gave the slightest wag with the tip of her tail. I put my hands up to the cage in case she wanted to come for a sniff. "Hi, beautiful," I cooed. The dogs behind me couldn't take it any more. They barked and howled and whined and begged for attention, too. I said hello to each of them, and when they stopped barking, my dog, *the one*, formerly known as Misty, let out a shy, but forceful "Woof." I knew I had found Winsome.

I took her information card to the adoption counter and began the process to bring home the new love of my life. Winsome would need to be spayed. She would also need a visit to the veterinarian after I took her home to make sure she was healthy. If there were any health related issues, I could bring Winsome back to the SPCA for a full refund. Before all that took place, I had to fill out a three-page questionnaire to make sure I could provide a stable, loving environment to a dog that had a perilous beginning to her life.

With my new job, I kept regular work hours and would be able to come home during lunch to take her on walks. I passed inspection. The adoption specialist recommended that I buy a crate to keep Winsome in during the day. I felt very uncomfortable with that idea as she had been kept in a cage for more than three weeks. I thought she deserved her freedom. This was her new house. Let her roam. The adoption specialist did not think this would be a good idea, but instead, recommended baby gates so Winsome could be enclosed in my galley kitchen while I was not at home. This I agreed to do.

A week passed, and finally, on April 12, 1994, I was able to bring Winsome home. She tentatively walked out of the doors of the SPCA with me. The new blue leash I bought her looked so pretty against her shiny black fur. I was armed with a five pound bag of the designer dog food they fed her. I was surprised that the SPCA didn't use a more moderately priced brand to feed all of their animals. Clearly, their mission was to provide a warm, loving, secure and healthy environment for these animals until they found new homes. I also had the number of the dog trainer that the SPCA highly recommended who taught some of her lessons on their campus. I was to start obedience lessons the following Saturday in order to see what Winsome really knew.

Her visit with the veterinarian the SPCA recommended determined Winsome was part Lab, part terrier and a few other things mixed in for good measure. She weighed in at forty-three pounds, had strong hips, solid build and all her adult teeth. The vet placed her age at about eighteen months. I was thrilled that she was so young. She was out of her puppy stage, yet I could enjoy many, many years with her.

GETTING TO KNOW YOU

While I was at home, Winsome now called Winn, had free rein of the house. She slept under my bed on a peach colored rug. Everywhere I went, she went. When I took a shower, she lay on the bathroom rug. When I'd pour myself a bowl of cereal, she'd be under foot in the kitchen. We quickly established a routine. I'd get up at 5:00 a.m. and take her for an hour walk through the neighborhood. I'd take a shower, leave for work and come home at lunch to walk her around the block. I'd come home from work at 4:30 and take her for another hour-long walk. We both began to get muscular. Winn really enjoyed my company.

After I'd had her for about a week, I noticed that she had very strong opinions about my abandoning her to go to work. I came home for her lunch time walk, and noticed she had chewed through the baby gate cordoning her off from the living room. I naively thought that she chewed the gate so she could have more access to her new house. Maybe the quarry tile floor was too cold and hard. Perhaps she just wanted to snooze on the couch. So, I took the gate away and went back to work. I immersed myself in my job, looking up, from time to time to gaze at the picture my mother took of Winn and me the day I brought her home from the SPCA.

When I came home that day, I couldn't open my front door all the way. I poked my head though to see what the problem may be. Winn had, in the course of three hours, destroyed my couch. The reason I couldn't open the door all the way was because the cushions had been taken off the couch, dismantled and shredded, and the stuffing blocked the doorway. There was foam and stuffing from one end of the first floor to the other. Winn was a very busy girl.

I took Winn for her walk and formulated a plan in my head. What was I going to do to help ease her into her new life? We came home, and I began the arduous task of cleaning up couch guts. I swept and tossed out remains for an hour. Winn watched with curiosity. I called the SPCA and asked for help. The help desk suggested that I call the dog trainer with whom I was to begin obedience classes in three days. The trainer was very kind and soothing and asked very intelligent questions. She wanted to get to know my dog and formulate a training plan that worked well for Winn and me. One of the questions she asked was how many times a day was I feeding Winn. I replied that she got fed in the morning, just as she had at the SPCA. The trainer suggested I feed Winn twice a day. Perhaps she was eating the couch because she was hungry. Why hadn't I thought of that?! Sheer brilliance! I was going to love taking Winn to this woman's obedience classes. The trainer left me with a parting comment—never let Winn see me bend over. If I needed to clean up after Winn or pick up anything on the floor, I should remove Winn from the area. The reason for this, the trainer explained, was so Winn would not see me in a submissive position.

The rest of that week proved more of the same. I'd come home dreading the mess that was in my living room. The couch was chewed down to the wooden frame in the back. With the trainer's advice in my head, I'd point to the mess, tell Winn she was a bad dog in a disappointed voice, put her in the powder room so she wouldn't see me clean the mess, and tidy up. Then we'd go for our walk. I couldn't wait until Saturday's training began.

ALPHA DOG

We were not the only ones at the training session that beautiful Saturday in April. Not all of the dogs had come from the SPCA, but most had. There were children who came to train their new dogs as the parents watched from the sidelines. Those dogs were so gentle as they bestowed joyous licks on the faces of their young charges. There was a golden retriever puppy that began his lesson being carsick from the long drive. The trainer assured the owner that the sickness would end soon, and that she should take him on short car trips at any opportunity and give plenty of praise and reassurance during the rides.

The trainer watched me as I handled Winn. Winn's muscles were evident in her chest and hips. She was strong and she was not pleased to be around other dogs and their humans. The trainer came up to us and Winn made a deep-throated sound. It was as though Winn wanted to growl, but thought better of it and swallowed it back. The trainer summed Winn up in a nutshell. She determined Winn was an alpha dog. Winn would not do well around other people and other dogs. I mentioned that Winn and I liked to walk for several miles each day and that I was considering walking her to a college spring festival about five miles from my house. The trainer implored me not to; saying the crowds would be more than Winn would be able to stand. Winn would be better off in quiet situations.

It dawned on me that Winn was not winsome at all. In fact, she was the opposite. She was a trouble maker. She snarled at the other dogs and wouldn't listen in class. I don't know why we weren't kicked out of class that first day. Private lessons may have been a better option for us. Perhaps the trainer was ready for a challenge. Maybe she had seen worse. I was relieved when, at the end of that first class, we were given a homework assignment and the reassuring words, "See you next week!"

Winn and I worked hard. She excelled at sitting, laying down and giving her paw. That last one was not taught in class, but by my mother. She needed serious improvement in staying in one place, not pulling on the leash and coming when called when off the leash. Because Winn was unruly, we only practiced her being off the leash during our lessons.

One day, because of a scheduling conflict, I had a semi-private lesson. There was just one other dog in the class and he was owned by an SPCA staff member. It was pouring down rain, and we met inside. It was more of a question and answer session that a lesson. It proved to be the most insightful day of my dog ownership. After three weeks of lessons and watching Winn as well as listening to the things I said, the trainer determined that Winn, at some time, had a bad experience with a male with facial hair who wore a uniform of some sort. Perhaps this man had even abused her. She also told me what the staff member in the lesson already knew. Winn was thanking me for giving her a second chance. Winn sensed that I had saved her and she was going to take it upon herself to protect me. It was her thank you to me.

As I looked back, I realized Winn shredded the mail when it came through the mail slot in the door. The neighbor with the beard tried to pet Winn, and she nipped him on the finger. The lawn service up the street wore uniforms and Winn tried to attack their riding lawn mower. It was a huge *eureka* moment for me.

Shortly afterward, my former flame came to the house with a truck and some buddies to move the remains of his short life with me out of the house. Since we always were cordial to each other I asked him to get rid of the remains of my couch as well. He said he'd do his best. Winn and I left for the afternoon to practice our lessons and to go to the pet store to buy a choke chain. The trainer assured me a choke chain was not cruel, but self- correcting. If the chain was put on correctly (the loop for the neck and the remainder of the chain shaped like the letter "P" for perfect) Winn would choke if she pulled, but when she heeled the chain would be loose.

I was looking forward to having the couch removed and mentally planned how I was going to rearrange the furniture. The trainer suggested removing all furniture from under the window so Winn couldn't jump up and have an anxiety attack whenever she saw the letter carrier walk by.

When we got home with the choke chain, dog treats and new pet bed, Winn and I discovered the offending couch was still in the living room. I was livid at my former flame's typical ambivalence. I called him up and asked why he hadn't taken the couch. He mumbled something about not having room in the truck, that it was too heavy, blah, blah, blah. Winn, sensing my anger, took her new dog bed and started shaking it until the little beads of stuffing started to roll on the floor. She was upset that I was upset. I knew immediately that I needed to calm down.

I took Winn for a walk so we could both relax. She pulled at every opportunity, and she'd choke herself. Then, along with the command "don't pull," she stopped pulling and stopped choking. It was the first time in the four weeks I owned her that my shoulder wasn't sore after our walk.

AND THEN THERE WERE THREE

The man who mowed my tiny lawn and helped me around the house offered to take my couch to the dump. I put Winn on the deck where she was happy to sun herself on the warm wood, and watched in amazement as it took four strong men to move the carcass of furniture. I forgot it was a sleeper sofa. Winn was not pleased to have four strangers to her in my house interacting with me. She could not protect me. She barked and scratched at the French doors separating the deck from the dining room the whole time the men tried to manipulate the couch through the door and into the back of the pick up truck. She gave them a menacing bark and growl as they pulled away. She was the protector from the deck.

Winn sniffed the area around where the couch used to be. She found residual foam from the cushions and took it in her mouth and shook her head vigorously. When Winn realized the couch was not coming back, she began chewing on the rails of the banister. A call to the trainer informed me that alum put on any surface she chewed on would stop the behavior in its tracks. That proved to be untrue. Winn quickly developed a liking for alum's bitter taste. She didn't mind the taste of bitter apple either.

Unbeknownst to me, Winn also chewed the phone cord in my bedroom. While I was sleeping, she was under the bed nibbling on the part of the cord that fell near her. I very rarely used that phone and had no idea anything was amiss. One evening, I got a call while I was reading in bed. As I was talking, the phone disconnected. The person whom I was speaking with was my friend who had wanted to set me up with her employer. We did actually go out on a date the previous October. I thought things went really well, but he never called me back. I didn't care now; I had a dog in my life. I didn't need anyone else. My friend was calling to ask if she could give her employer my phone number again, as he had asked her for it. When the phone disconnected, she took that as my answer. I called her back and told her that I didn't think he liked me because I never heard back from him. She assured me he had just been busy, so I told her to give him my number.

I didn't think any more of our conversation and had completely forgotten about replacing the chewed up phone cord in the bedroom. Winn and I continued our walks and obedience lessons. She was very sensitive to my needs and could sense if I was nervous. If we walked by another dog, she'd bark and lunge and then cough and hack as she choked herself. I was nervous because I thought she would lunge and bark at another dog or human or mail truck. She never disappointed me.

One night while I was reading in bed, the phone rang. I answered and the call disconnected. Since this was way before the invention of caller ID, I had to hope the person on the other end would call back. He did. It was Ken, the man whom my friend wanted me to date. I handled the phone very carefully and asked for his number in case the phone call got dropped. I explained I got a dog that was going through a chewing phase. Ken laughed and said he, too, had a dog, and he remembered those days well. We agreed to another date. I was reluctant to leave Winn behind, as we were always together except when I went to work. Ken agreed to come to the house for dinner. We made the arrangements while the phone mercifully cooperated. He was to come over on May 12.

Everything was planned. I had fresh tulips in the vase, a nice bottle of wine chilling, and a wonderful chicken dish ready to be cooked. The doorbell rang. I had forgotten how handsome Ken was. Winn barked, but he told her it was okay and gingerly sidestepped by her. I apologized for her rude behavior and explained how I had adopted her the month before and that she was very protective of me. I poured us each a glass of wine and sat down. Winn lay down and moped. Then she stood up, went into the dining room and tinkled on the floor. I was shocked and embarrassed and went immediately into the dining room to clean up the puddle. Forgetting that the trainer told me never to bend over in front of Winn, I knelt down. Winn watched my submissive position from the living room and promptly bit Ken on the leg, tearing his pants.

Ken calmly asked me to call off my dog, which I did, of course. I don't really know how we managed to have such a good time getting reacquainted after Winn's stellar performance. We made arrangements for another date, this time at his house, where I would meet his dog.

CRUISE CONTROL

I took Winn out to my parent's house in the country. They had an enclosed area behind their house and invited us for some doggie socialization. They had plenty of treats on hand to help her feel comfortable in her new surroundings.

Things were going well until Winn saw the horses. She must have thought they were a pack of dogs and went into her full alpha routine. She barked. She growled. She bared her teeth. The horses got antsy, and Winn would not let up. Even after I brought her into the house, she barked her menacing bark through the window. The horses passed with their ears pinned back. Winn certainly knew how to ruin a quiet day at the farm.

We were asked to leave, although, we were going to excuse ourselves anyway.

The ride home to my house could be long or longer depending on the route. Winn and I decided to bypass the highways and take the back roads. Winn rode shotgun, and she settled into her seat enjoying the view and fresh air. She got bored and lay down on the seat and fell asleep. I rubbed her head and marveled at how innocent she looked while she was sleeping. Who could believe this barkoholic could look so calm and peaceful?

We approached civilization, and our country road met the interstate. While sitting at a red light, I happened to look in the rearview mirror and saw a red Nissan Sentra missing its license plates fast approaching my car. There were four large men in their late teens or early twenties in the car, and they abruptly stopped behind me, rolled down their windows and started swinging baseball bats. I was terrified. I was about to run the light when it changed to green. I sped through the intersection only to be stopped by another red light. There were cars in front of me and in the next lane. The baseball bat swingers were right behind me. I was stuck. Winn sensed my fear and sat up. She started growling and then barked her head off. She barked so loudly the drivers of the cars around me looked up. The car in front of me saw my dilemma and drove though the intersection in order to let me go past. I sped through the red light, only to be followed by these maniacs. Winn kept her head out the window barking evilly at the Nissan. The car eventually gave up chase and passed me waving their baseball bats in the air as they did.

I often wonder if things would have turned out differently if Winn wasn't in the car that day.

DOG EAT DOG WORLD

I did meet my date's dog. Her name was Dixie and she was part beagle and part Lab. She had this big body on stubby legs. She was slightly incontinent from a botched spaying procedure when she was a puppy. She smelled a bit like urine and dog breath. It wasn't an entirely bad combination once you got to know her. She had such a happy expression on her face, and when she wagged her tail it was in big swooping circles not side to side. She had hip displasia that left her unable to sit. She had her own armchair that she was the queen of. She would lie there all day until she heard any sound that reminded her of food. When she heard a pot or pan or can opener she jumped off her chair like she had no handicap at all. The three of us enjoyed steak that night.

After dinner the three of us went into the living room. Ken and I sat on the floor and gave Dixie some love. When he leaned over to give me a kiss, Dixie would have none of it and promptly got up, lay on top of me and intercepted. We laughed at the jealous nature of our dogs and decided to arrange a puppy play date.

I called my trainer with the news of this upcoming event, and she advised we have the play date at Dixie's house to level out the playing field. An alpha dog would not necessarily feel inclined to defend a territory that was not their own. She also recommended my taking Winn on a long walk and implementing a vigorous training session so her mind and body would be tired.

Winn and I got to Dixie's house, and we went right into the backyard. Dixie had a huge and beautifully manicured backyard that was fenced in. Winn and Dixie were introduced and the barking began. Dixie wasn't much of a barker, but she could hold up her end of the conversation. Winn antagonized Dixie, and Dixie got fed up in a hurry. Winn ran circles around Dixie in the big backyard. Dixie stood and watched, perplexed. Winn came up to Dixie to taunt her. Dixie barked loudly and lay down. We watched this initiation from the living room window near the sun porch. From there, we could intercede if there was a problem. After a few minutes, we realized Winn was missing. We went outside and found Winn; she was underneath Dixie. Dixie took matters into her own hands and decided to show this little upstart dog a lesson using her best defense. Dixie heaved her big Lab body on Winn and squished her. Winn was okay, definitely stunned, but she was okay. Dixie got up, went through her doggie door to the porch and deemed the play date over.

SUMMER LOVIN'

Winn earned her diploma at obedience school, but I had the trainer's number on speed dial for the never ending questions I seemed to have about Winn's behavior. Classes were not in session during the hot summer months, but she was only ever a phone call away.

Winn and Dixie continued to have occasional play dates. Winn never bit Ken again. We all seemed to be getting along quite well. Ken and I decided to go sailing for a weekend. His cousin often took care of Dixie, but we were afraid to leave Winn at his house, too. She was so aggressive that 1) we didn't think she would let his cousin in the front door, and 2) she might attack Dixie.

I decided to kennel Winn. I took her to a farm way out in the country almost to the Pennsylvania border. I decided to board her at this particular location because they agreed to give her almost exclusive one on one attention, and it was the last place I called that had any openings on a busy summer weekend. Off we went to this bucolic setting surrounded by weeping willows, fenced-in areas for running, a pond for swimming and piped in music for relaxation. I went sailing without a care in the world knowing Winn was in good hands. She was in very good hands. She looked wonderful when I came to pick her up at 6:00 in the morning so I could bring her home and get to work by 8:30, but Winn did not feel as good as she looked.

She was physically sick as soon as we got to the car, and I had to stop several times on the way home so she could be sick. Winn and I got home, and I gave her a quick walk to make sure her illness had ended. It hadn't. I just came to terms that there might be a huge mess to clean up when I came home at lunch time. Miraculously there wasn't. Winn waited until we went for our walk and got sick outside. I called the trainer to ask if I should take Winn to the vet. She advised me to wait. If Winn was drinking water and eating a little bit of food, she'd probably be okay. The trainer suggested it was separation anxiety. Putting Winn in a kennel was like her life back at the SPCA. While the care was wonderful, it wasn't the same care she had known to get from me. I felt the guilt-o-meter surge to full tilt with that little nugget of information.

Ken and I went to my college friend's wedding in Connecticut. Winn went back to the kennel for two weeks this time. I called the owners of the kennel frequently to make sure she was okay. The trainer and the owners of the kennel agreed that I should not talk to Winn on the phone as that would just confuse her and make her anxious. The wedding was wonderful, Ken's and my relationship forged ahead, and Winn was fine when I picked her up from the kennel.

Toward the end of the summer I started getting blinding headaches. I couldn't see clearly. I drove through stop signs. I fainted on several occasions. I took handfuls of acetaminophen. I took to my bed. It was by the grace of God I was able to drive myself to work and home each day. Winn's walks were interrupted. Except for quick strolls around the block, we didn't go out. I lay in my bed with the shades drawn. Winn lay under my bed and did not move until I did. She looked at me with her big brown eyes as if to say she wanted to make me feel better. She would do anything for me. I petted her soft fur and cried from the pain and cried at the fact that Winn the ferocious beast was really a kind-hearted soul who wanted to shoulder my burden.

A trip to the neurologist's office and an unexceptional CT scan determined I was having a reaction to some medicine I was taking. The day I stopped taking the medicine I felt better. Winn and I were able to enjoy our walks again, even in the oppressive heat of Baltimore in August. I'll never forget how much Winn loved me during that time.

SO HAPPY TOGETHER

By the end of October, Ken and I decided to take our relationship even further, and he asked me to marry him. He had mentioned the idea of me living with him, but having lived that disaster twice with the same person in two different states, I declined stating that I would only ever live with a man if I were engaged. Ken purchased for me the engagement ring I had been periodically going into the jewelry store to try on since I was eighteen years old.

Winn and I packed up our things and moved a mile up the road into Ken's house. Winn and Dixie were pretty friendly to each other, but Dixie was not thrilled to be upstaged by a new human and her alpha dog. Ken and I tried to provide the dogs with lots of walks and treats. The first morning I woke up in my new home I found that Dixie had gone to the bathroom all over the dining room floor. There was no place for me to walk that wasn't covered with her "presents."

It took me an hour to clean the floor while trying not to gag. It was her welcome gift to Winn and me.

I left the dogs outside for the day and went to work. When I came home there were several messages on our machine about Winn's nonstop barking. She could see our neighbors and anyone who walked up and down the back alley through our chain link fence. When she wasn't barking, she was digging to get out and show our neighbors what she was really all about. Our next door neighbor was terrified of Winn and her husband asked us to get rid of our bark-o-maniac. We opted instead to replace our chain link fence with a six foot high wooden fence set on railroad ties so Winn could not see our neighbors or dig out to meet them. Our neighbors were hurt at first that we built such a high fence, but in the end, they enjoyed their privacy, and I think Winn felt a little less anxious not having to protect us from everyone or everything she saw.

One of our gates that was attached to the side of our house remained the chain link style. One day Ken got a call from a neighbor up the street from us asking who Winn's veterinarian was and if her rabies shot was up to date. Winn had bitten her twelve-year- old son and had broken the skin. Ken called me at work and told me what had happened. He suggested that we may need to euthanize Winn since she was so vicious. I wanted to get all the information from the woman who called before taking Winn back to the SPCA.

I called the neighbor and began by apologizing for the incident and assured her that Winn's shots were up to date. I explained that I had rescued Winn from the SPCA six months before, and she felt a tremendous need to protect us. She told me that her son and two other boys from the neighborhood were taunting Winn. They stuck their faces up to the chain link gate and barked at her. She got back in their faces and barked. They stuck their fingers through the gate, and that's when she bit the boy. That afternoon, I stopped by the pet store and bought a "Beware of Dog" sign to put on both gates to the yard. After that, both dogs stayed inside until Ken and I got home.

PITTER PATTER

Winn seemed very interested in my every motion. She had settled enough into a routine in her new home that she could relax a little. Leaving her indoors certainly helped her anxiety. She only needed to save us from the letter carrier and the gas and electric meter readers. She'd bark ferociously at the other passing dogs. Dixie didn't care about the other dogs. She was in her armchair and all was right with the world until her next meal arrived. Winn felt she needed to protect Dixie, too, and Dixie let her. As a result, Winn became a little aloof. She stopped pacing so much and started napping, albeit with one eye open. If we were in the living room, she might be in the dining room. But one day I noticed when I would sit on the couch, Winn was either on the couch with me or lying on the floor next to me. I'd take a shower, and Winn was waiting for me to come out. It was just like it was when I first brought her home from the SPCA. She looked at me with this worried expression, and I wondered if she knew something I didn't know. It turns out, she did. I was pregnant!

By the end of November I stopped working. Winn and Dixie were thrilled. They got walks all the time, and when I got hungry, which seemed to be all the time, they got snacks. For them, life was wonderful. Walking them together was like flying a kite. They each were on retractable leashes. Winn was in my left hand, Dixie in my right, and they would criss-cross each other to sniff the smells on the other side of the sidewalk. We got tangled on a few occasions. They loved it.

The winter was long and cold, and we all stayed indoors. Dixie hated to get her feet wet. She had beagle legs, but she also had Labrador webbed feet. Her feet, in theory, were perfect for water, but her brain disagreed. We would take turns digging a path in the snow for the dogs to go. Dixie insisted we put towels down in the path so her feet stayed dry.

Spring came and Winn noticed that my formerly flat stomach was big and round. She loved to jump up and put her paws on my expanding girth. In March I was put on bed rest, so Winn went on bed rest, too. She would lie next to me, only getting up to protect the house from the letter carrier or other dogs walking by. In May, I was given the green light to resume light activity. I would walk the dogs in the morning, run an errand, eat, watch TV, take them for a second walk, take a nap, figure out dinner, walk them for a third time and be in bed by 9:00 p.m. Neighbors that I didn't know at that time later told me they referred to me as the "pregnant dog walker."

Winn had not changed her need to protect us, and quite frankly I was worried to death that she was going to harm the baby in some way. I didn't want to send her back to the SPCA just because of my fears. I placed a hormonally induced tearful call to the trainer and explained my concerns. She said my worries were justified. She told me that Ken and I absolutely needed to do two things to make the adjustment of having a baby in the house easier on both dogs. The first one was that Ken needed to bring the first blanket the baby was wrapped in home for the dogs to smell. While they sniffed it, Ken was to pet them and give them treats. Winn and Dixie would equate this new smell with love and food. The second thing we had to do was fill a small container with dog treats and keep it by the front door. Family and friends who came to admire the baby or bring food would first take a treat from the basket and give one to each dog—the dogs would get the attention before the baby.

On June 5, 1995, our son, Alex, was born. My sick fantasy that the dogs would play tug of war with the baby proved to be unfounded. Winn and Dixie both retreated anytime Alex cried, which was often at first. The dogs loved getting the attention before Alex or I did. Winn barked her head off whenever the doorbell rang. For a while we just put out a sign on the front door saying "Don't Ring the Doorbell, Just Come On In" if we knew people were going to come over. Winn took Alex into the fold and protected him, too.

RUNNING BUDDIES

Alex liked being in his backpack, but he loved his stroller the best. When he was ten months old, Winn and I would take Alex on long walks through the neighborhood. Winn would always walk diagonally in front so she could use her body to protect Alex and me from another person or animal. That April the flowers were in full bloom, the air was sweet and the bunnies came out to play. Winn discovered that chasing bunnies was fun! The first time she did it, she pulled Alex and me into a run. Alex shrieked with delight. When I regained control of Winn and we slowed to a walk, Alex cried. He wanted to run. Winn was happy to oblige. We ran on the hilly streets of our neighborhood. Alex giggled, Winn chased small animals, and I silently screamed in pain.

After a couple of weeks of this I bought a jogging stroller, and Winn, Alex and I ran daily. It was exhilarating! Dixie excused herself from this activity, but was happy to accompany us on our slow-paced evening strolls.

The great thing about running was Winn didn't bark. She just led us on our journeys. We would see other dogs and other humans, but unless she stopped, overcome by a new aroma, she just forged ahead.

Although I knew it would be cruel and unusual punishment to run everywhere were went, all day and all night long, I was thrilled and relieved to find that Winn was capable of being quiet during waking hours.

LEARNING CURVES

I don't know if Winn and Dixie ever really liked each other, or just merely tolerated each other. They were very different. Dixie lived to eat and get her belly rubbed. She was only interested in us for those two needs. Most of the time she would lie in her chair and sleep. She liked her walks and would arthritically attempt to jump up and down when she saw the leash. Winn, on the other hand, ate to live. I remember her going for three days with one bowl of food. She wasn't sick or picky. She just wasn't a big eater. Winn liked attention too, but mostly on her terms.

When Alex started eating solid food, Dixie must have thought she'd died and gone to heaven. She had her own buffet, right on the kitchen floor. Winn, too, quickly figured out that people food was a much better option to anything in her bowl. The dogs loved the sound of the tray snapping in place to the highchair. They knew they were going to dine on the finest cuisine of Cheerios, strained peas, sweet potatoes, and pureed green beans. Alex loved the performance, and I never had to get the vacuum cleaner out as long as a dog was around.

Dixie had her own space. There was her smelly old armchair in the living room that no other animal or human dared to sit on, but she also had the sun porch. If the dogs were inside the house, they could both join us on the porch. The porch had a door leading to the backyard, and it also had a doggie door. This was Dixie's door. Winn was terrified of anything hitting her face, so she would not use the doggie door. If Dixie wanted to get away from Winn, she would go through the door. Dixie could go in or out, but Winn had to stay in one place or the other. Winn had her own space as well. The terrier in her made her an excellent jumper, and she claimed Ken's and my bed for snoozing and for a lookout perch to guard us from yet another angle. The problem with that was Winn would become very anxious protecting us from the letter carrier, so she would destroy our pillows. Amazingly, Ken and I did not learn from our mistakes and kept putting the pillows back on the bed out of habit. When we had to sleep with our heads on the mattress, we finally remembered to put the new pillows in the closet.

Winn and Dixie had a few things in common, though. They both had an excellent command of the English language. Dixie was very well trained if there was no food in her reach. Ken took it upon himself to train her, and he did a wonderful job. Winn had to be trained well. You can't leave anything to chance with a vicious dog, one false move and someone could get hurt. But their vocabulary went far beyond basic commands. They knew the words treat, walk, tummy yummy, ride in the car, go to bed, and let's get a snack. We could interpret their barks to determine if they were excited or upset, but we never did get the hang of Doggese.

Winn and Dixie also taught us how to fetch. We'd get a toy, throw it and say "go get it." They'd just lie on the floor and watch as we retrieved their toy for them. Ken and I, as it turned out, were well trained, too.

MIX AND MATCH

In the fall of 1997, Ken and I had another son, Tim. Winn and Dixie seemed used to the routine of having a baby underfoot. Dixie would barely move from her chair, and any visitors would need to take a treat from the basket and bring it to her. Winn slunk upstairs and jumped on our bed to get away from the activity. Dixie was very uncomfortable; her poor joints just weren't up to the challenge of carrying her hefty weight around any more than necessary. Winn was tired, and she paced the floors day and night. When we were all together in the evenings, she finally relaxed.

That winter, Dixie's organs were failing her, and Ken decided to take her to the veterinarian. Alex and I gave her lots of hugs, and Winn came down from the bedroom and gave Dixie a full-body sniff. Then they left, and Dixie didn't come home. We buried her ashes under a dogwood tree in the back yard. The boys still refer to it as Dixie's tree.

By the spring, Ken couldn't stand it anymore. He needed another dog. A puppy. I had my hands full and couldn't fathom taking care of a two year old, an infant and a puppy while Ken worked fourteen-hour days. Ken's mind was made up. "We'll make it work," he said. "This'll be great!" he enthused.

By the summer, he knew the breed he wanted to get and exchanged emails with breeders in the area. Ken read books about the Portuguese water dog. Our neighbor had one, and she seemed like a lot of work. They walked her for miles each day. At the age of eight, she still was all puppy. Our neighbors would say "Oh, she's so calm, now. You should have seen her before." Oh boy.

On November 8, 1998, Lucky was born. The breeder called the house while Ken was at work to give us the news. I was blunt with the breeder. I told him we had an alpha female at home and that I was very uncomfortable bringing a puppy into the fold. I told him I essentially had two babies in the house already, and wasn't sure how or what they'd do with a puppy. The breeder was very direct and informative. Lucky was the runt of the litter. He was muscled out of the group by the other puppies, and the breeder bottle fed him. Lucky was so tiny and frail, they didn't think he'd make it through the first night. He did, and that's how he got his name. Lucky would always be small and had an omega temperament. The breeder thought Winn and Lucky could get along fine, but if he was wrong, we could always return Lucky anytime.

My husband was ecstatic, but he couldn't pick Lucky up for eight weeks. Ken was like a kid in a candy store. He bought all the supplies he thought a puppy would need. I was no help. Having adopted Winn when she was eighteen months old, I never went through puppyhood. Dixie was a puppy fifteen years ago. Who could remember? Ken drove five hours down to Virginia Beach to get Lucky. Alex wanted so badly to go, but there was no way a two and a half year old could be in the car for a total of ten hours. I don't know many adults who can do that either. Later that evening, Ken came home with Lucky. He was a little ball of fluff. Alex wanted to hold him. Winn wanted to eat him.

We went through a few hours of "Now What?". After I put the boys to bed, Ken and I tried to deal with the issue that a puppy was going to be a lot of work. We were both exhausted, and realized everything would be clearer in the morning. Winn went upstairs with us and Lucky went into his crate in the living room. As soon as we got settled in bed, the crying started. I checked on the boys, but discovered it was Lucky. This was his first night away from his brothers and sisters and parents, and he was so lonely. The breeder told us to keep him in his crate. Lucky would come to know his crate as his own space that he could go to chill out, but we needed to make him comfortable while he was there. I brought the kitchen timer into the living room. I remembered someone saying the ticking of a timer was similar to a mother's heartbeat. Apparently, Lucky's mother's heart didn't sound that way because Lucky was still crying. I went upstairs and told Ken how sad Lucky was. Ken said that maybe Lucky would whine himself to sleep. I hated when the boys cried at night. I never let them cry themselves to sleep. If they cried, there was a problem. I couldn't let Lucky cry either. Ken was exhausted from the long drive and had already fallen back to sleep. I took my pillow and some blankets and camped out in the living room with Lucky. He stuck his big paw through a slat in the crate. I put my hand on his paw and started to stroke it. He calmed down. When I stopped petting him and fell asleep, he started to cry again. All night I held his fuzzy paw in mine. He finally slept.

I was not the blue bird of happiness the next day to be sure. I need my sleep. Ken, however was very refreshed, and went about finding a trainer for Lucky. I suggested the SPCA. I said that Winn's trainer was fabulous, though I stopped myself from saying "Look at how great Winn turned out."

Ken found a trainer who would come out to the house. Winn let the trainer come in with barely a growl, so I felt reassured that he could command respect from dogs. We learned how to teach Lucky the basics. He became house broken, learned to sit and lay down. He did not easily learn how to walk on a leash and how to leave Winn alone. Winn did an excellent job teaching him the latter. Lucky learned very quickly not go near her food, her bed or the toys I had bought her in hopes that she would one day like to play. If he did, Winn gave him a warning growl. If Lucky ignored the warning, which he almost always did at first, Winn would grab him by the scruff of the neck. She didn't hurt him, but she scared the heck out of him, and Lucky would retreat to his crate.

IF THIS IS THE OMEGA, WHAT'S THE ALPHA?

Lucky grew, and his energy was never ending. He got into everything. Toilet paper was shredded, the children's stuffed animals were unstuffed, and shoes were ruined. He loved to play.

Lucky and Winn spent a lot of time outside in the backyard. Winn taught Lucky how to dig holes in the grass. Lucky was an avid learner. He also dug holes in the mulch, the boys' sandbox and in the flower beds. I watched with horror out my bathroom window as Lucky dug up all of my tulip bulbs in the span of about thirty seconds.

Ken was in Florida for a meeting during the Great Dig. I called him and told him that I was fed up and forced to use drastic measures. Ken was so sure that meant I was going to call the breeder to send Lucky back to Virginia. Actually, I placed a call to Invisible Fence and had them install an underground electric fence to prevent both dogs from going into my flower beds or out of the front yard. The premise for the fence was simple. The dogs would wear a collar that would emit a signal to let them know they were approaching the fence (aka: the danger zone). If they got too close to the fence, they'd get shocked. The shock was calibrated by weight and personality, so twenty-pound Lucky and fifty-pound Winn got the same sensation. I felt the shock on my finger, and it was only a little worse than touching a lamp after walking across the carpet in stocking feet. The training was simple. I put each dog on their leash, one at a time, walked them up to the area near the fence. When they heard the signal, I told them "be careful" and then gently pulled them away. Training sessions were done three times a day in increments of three for a week.

Both dogs quickly learned to avoid the signal. Winn hated the high pitched noise. She did get shocked once and never needed the collar again while she was outside. Lucky got shocked on a few occasions. When he got something in his mind, he just couldn't let it go. Sometimes the devil made him do it, and he had to dig. He couldn't stop himself, but the collar could.

It was a spring with no flowers in the gardens, but boundaries were established.

JUMPING FOR JOY

The bed in Ken's and my room is far from the floor. Whenever Alex or Tim wanted to get on the bed, they would get a running start from the bathroom and take a flying leap. Winn made it look easy. She just stood at the side of the bed, made her calculations and jumped. Lucky was befuddled. He'd run and miss, and he'd stand and miss. Over and over, we'd hear the thud of dismay, and Lucky's cry of frustration as he yet, again, missed the bed. He was nothing if not persistent.

We loved watching TV in the "big bed" The boys would jump up, Winn would jump up, and Ken and I would climb in. Poor Lucky, he had to be lifted up if he wanted to join us. One evening, we all went upstairs to the big bed to resume our routine. As we brushed our teeth, Lucky stared at the bed. It was as though he was sizing it up. He came into the bathroom, turned around, scampered to the bed and jumped. He landed on the bed! We all cheered for him and gave him pats. Winn was not thrilled that Lucky could get up on "her" bed. We all snuggled and loved up the dogs, congratulating Lucky and commiserating with Winn.

The next morning, Ken and I went downstairs to start breakfast. Winn followed shortly thereafter with the boys. We ate breakfast, did the dishes and asked the dogs if they were ready for their "walkie, walkie." Lucky barked and barked. We went upstairs and discovered that Lucky hadn't learned how to jump *off* the bed.

Not too long after, I'd come home from running errands and hear the sound of both dogs jumping off the bed to greet me. What a homecoming!

BEGGING VERSUS BEING CUTE

Winn had her reputation as being the "mean one" down to a science. Play dates hinged on the location of the dogs. If friends came over to play and the dogs were inside, the play date was either in the basement area or outside. If the gang wanted to play in the living room, the dogs were banished to the outside or the bedroom.

Why did Lucky have to leave? Well it wasn't because of his personality. He loves being around people and other dogs. He wags his tail, makes a welcoming bark that sounds like a train, and brings the guest a present, usually one of our shoes. He is the mayor of our community greeting each one of our neighbors with a "woof" and a wag. Lucky also loves food as much as he does people.

There is no plate, bowl, dish or cup that Lucky hasn't at one time or another gotten into. He figured out early on that mealtime is the best part of the day. I don't know how this behavior transpired. I know we used food as a reward for both dogs for training purposes. After meals we would take a few pieces of our leftovers and bring it into the kitchen to give the dogs, but I just don't remember how it came that Lucky started barking and yipping and staring us down at mealtime.

Winn did not teach him this behavior. She liked her people food, for sure, but she had a different technique. She went for "cute." She'd put her paw on your leg and look at you with her soulful brown eyes as if to say, "Hi, I'd like some of your food, please." Then she'd leave us alone. She'd go upstairs to her bed, or climb on the sofa in the living room. Lucky would whine away, irritating us all in the process. Winn would come back in, repeat the process, and retreat. Lucky's whines would become high-pitched yips that made us yell to him to knock it off. After dinner, Winn would come into the kitchen and wait for her treat. Lucky would take your finger with the food.

Sometimes the boys would take a snack into the living room and draw or play at the table with their food dangerously close to both dogs' noses. Lucky would immediately go for the kill, so to speak. The snack was gone in a New York minute, and Lucky would be scolded and sent away. Winn, on the other hand would feign complete disinterest, walk by the table and gingerly take the snack. Like a person on the first day of a diet, she knew she shouldn't indulge, but snuck a taste anyway. The boys thought Winn was adorable. Here she was, interacting with the family, her defenses were down, and she felt comfortable enough to break the rules. Whenever Winn took one of the boys' treats, they'd say, "Awww, Winn's being cute again."

BECOMING MY DOG

For as long as I can remember, I have been a pacifist. I have always felt uncomfortable being in situations where there is discord. Whenever there is a problem, the Libra in me desperately tries to see both sides of the situation and bring harmony to the environment. I try never to start a fight, and if my boys are arguing, it is almost impossible for me to sit on the sidelines while they work it out. The older they get, the more Alex and Tim request I stay out of it, but it is so hard. Leaving the room is a necessity.

I am the peacekeeper. For years, people have asked me my opinion on how to keep relationships, friendships, or work relationships going smoothly. I never have a definitive answer, as each situation is different, but I always listen and encourage my audience to do the same. Most times people just want to know that their gripe, no matter how insignificant, is recognized.

It seems odd that a peacekeeping pacifist such as me would have a bully for a dog. I should have a kind dog, maybe one that cocks its head just so when a person speaks to look as though it is really interested in what is being said. Maybe a dog that offers a lick on the nose in reassurance. Nope, Winn never did any of that. I don't think she ever licked anyone except for herself during her grooming rituals.

Winn was always anxious. If a person sneezed more that once or coughed, she'd growl. Not in a way that offered any concern for the person making the offending sound, but more along the lines of being threatened by a sound she didn't recognize. If Winn sensed I was stressed out or worried about something, she'd get a furrow in between her eyebrows. Soothing words from me, then eventually the rest of the family, would allow her to relax her facial muscles.

Winn always protected us. I learned to protect us too. It started when the boys were small. I have always been fiercely protective of my husband and two sons. Probably as protective as Winn has always been, but I don't bite. I will growl, however. Don't purposely hurt my family with your words or your actions or I will let you know, usually in the form of a letter. Even today, my boys will tell me about a problem with someone, but they may preface it by saying, "Don't worry, Mom, you don't need to write a letter." Concerns about perceived injustices to my family have even caused worry furrows between my eyebrows. Fortunately, I know Botox.

Being anxious and concerned for our family's well-being is not always easy, and it can be absolutely exhausting. Winn would growl, bark and threaten, then go upstairs to the safety of her bed and sleep. When she couldn't sleep because of her anxiety, she would climb under our bed and eat the wood frame. Sometimes a kind word and some rubs would make her stop eating our bed. Other times I had to give her a "doggie downer" so she could relax. I, too, take to my bed after a long day of protecting my family. If I can't sleep, I think about how fortunate I am to have a family to take care of.

I can't help but think that Winn felt that way, too.

HAPPY DANCE

When I used to work ridiculously long hours in retail, days off were something to celebrate. It didn't matter if the day was spent doing laundry or paying bills or vacuuming—I wasn't at work. One time I looked at the store's work schedule and saw that I was off from Friday through Monday. After I processed that I might actually get a life outside of retail, I waved my arms up in the air, jumped in small circles and sang, "Happy dance, I'm doing the happy dance, cuz I don't have to work till Tuesday." This got repeated until I was hoarse and dizzy. I've done the happy dance a lot since that day. I just change the words around to fit the occasion. I've taught my family to do the Happy Dance. My kids still look at me like I'm a complete moron, but they do their dance in their own way. The important thing is to recognize a good thing and be happy about it.

Winn loved her walks. She sniffed everything. She had so

much energy when she was younger and, even when she was seven and arthritis began to settle into her right hip joint, insisted on walking for miles. Our reward for the long walks would be a trip to our community's stream. She would walk into the water, go chest high, stick her nose under the water and snort. She would do this repeatedly until she cooled off. When she came out of the water, she'd shake and go into a neighbor's lawn and roll in the grass. She'd roll back and forth, snorting and panting and scooting her body on its side with her back legs. It was Winn's Happy Dance.

Winn always found a reason and a place for the Happy Dance. The early morning grass might have dew or frost on it, and she'd roll in it. She might just roll in the grass to seize the day. She always had a huge smile on her face while lying in the grass doing her dance.

Lucky never understood Winn's dance. Her interruption of their walks unsettled his natural balance. He would bark at her and go over and nudge her, as if to let her know she was doing the walk wrong. This is not to say that Lucky isn't a dancer. In fact Lucky does a great Happy Dance. He always does his when the whole family is together. He rolls onto his back and kicks his paws up in the air and moans in delight. At meal time, Lucky adds music to his repertoire. He'll sing along with the can opener and yip words of encouragement for me to fill the bowls as full as possible.

There is always a wonderful reason to do the Happy Dance.

BEACH BOUND

When my husband and I decided to buy a beach house, there were a lot of variables we considered to make this the perfect long-term investment for us. We wanted a house that was roomy enough for the four of us, but not too big. We wanted to be on the bay. The house needed to have a deeded boat slip. Ken was a life long sailor and thought a power boat would be fun for fishing, knee boarding, and tooling around the bay. Also, as importantly as anything else, our house had to be in a community that would be safe for the boys and the dogs with plenty of grass and sidewalks. In the summer of 2005, after intensely searching for three years, we found the perfect house. It met all of our criteria and the community also boasted pools and tennis courts as well as many cul-de-sacs for plenty of safe walks with the dogs. There was also a pond filled with ducks and geese.

When we moved into the house that September, we left

the dogs at home so we could acclimate ourselves to our new surroundings. As we walked into town or on the docks or around the neighborhood, all four of us kept saying how much the dogs would love being at the beach. We waited until October to bring them down because at that point the beach is open to dogs. Winn excitedly got into the car and settled into her spot in the back. Lucky was not thrilled at all. Most of his trips in the car involved an appointment with the vet or groomer. He shook, he moaned, he threw up. It was a very long drive to the shore.

When we reached our destination, Lucky was relieved to have his feet touch solid ground. Winn was ready for a "walkie." We promptly took the dogs to explore their new neighborhood. They sniffed and snorted, Winn did the Happy Dance repeatedly, and Lucky yipped and jumped up and down. We took them to the dock. There the dogs discovered the most amazing thing ever. It was goose poop.

They sniffed it, ate it, rolled in it and repeated the ritual. We could not get them away from the stuff. While I never could get Winn to stop barking on command, she did obey all of my other commands—until now. Lucky listened to some commands and ignored the rest. He was in ignorance mode big time. We finally were able to drag them away from this Eastern Shore delicacy and hose them off. For the rest of the weekend, they were not allowed on the docks.

This did not stop them from enjoying themselves in other ways, however. They quickly adapted to the routine we established the first weekend we came down. The first order of business was to walk down to the doughnut shop. The boys grabbed their scooters, Ken and I each took a dog, and off we went. The dogs sniffed every blade of grass, fence post and tree for a half a mile. By the time we caught up with the boys, they were patiently waiting outside the doughnut shop, hungry and thirsty. Ken went in with Alex and Tim while I held Lucky and Winn's leashes. Winn sat politely while Lucky greeted all the passersby hoping for a free sample. With doughnuts and coffee in hand, we made our way back home to eat the feast on our deck. Winn and Lucky forgot about any other smell except for the one in the bags the boys were carrying. We got home in record time.

After breakfast that first full day with the dogs, we walked them further past the doughnut shop to the beach. They both always loved the sandbox at home, so we just knew their beach experience would be a great one. They did not disappoint. Lucky chased his ball, Winn chased the sea foam. They ran and frolicked and played for an hour. I had brought bottled water with me figuring the dogs would be eating a lot of sand, and I poured some water on their mouths and noses, but they didn't seem interested. After one last dip in the ocean for the dogs and the boys, we walked the half mile back to the house. We got just past the doughnut shop and into the grass when Winn did her Happy Dance. Lucky just looked at her and lay down beside her. Winn got up, but Lucky stayed in one spot. He got up and we walked a little further. Winn did her Dance and Lucky lay down again. Finally we got home where they took a long cool drink and fell asleep on the couch, like bookends, until dinner time. After that day, we drove them to the beach and back.

That first year, we went to the beach about every other weekend no matter what the weather was. Lucky very quickly equated the car with the beach and never got sick in the car again. One weekend in late October, there was a hurricane in Florida and the rain came up the coast, and it was warm but wet. The dogs didn't care. They loved to walk, roll, look for goose poop, and play on the beach. Alex and Tim were good sports about joining Ken or me on these drenching outings. The boys wore their swim suits and liked being in the rain with the dogs.

At one point, the rain had subsided, and Tim and I decided to run a couple of errands. Winn quickly escaped out the front door and sat by the car. I don't know if she thought we were leaving for good, or if she just wanted to be included on the road trip. We drove to the local gourmet store to figure out dinner. We left Winn in the car with the window down a bit. She was sleeping and didn't wake up when we got back in the car to make our next stop. Tim and I went to a sundries store to look around as a distraction from a mostly rainy day. We were in the store for about fifteen minutes, mindful of the sleeping dog in the car. When Tim and I got ready to exit the store, we noticed it had started raining again—hard. We ran to the car and Tim went to get in on his side, but Winn was there. Tim motioned for Winn to move over, but she sat firmly in Tim's spot. We looked up and remembered that we had left the window down a bit. Winn's side of the car was soaking wet. She didn't want to sit there. She wanted to be dry. Poor Tim had to sit in the puddle in the seat until we got home. We remarked at how brilliant Winn was.

SLIPPING AWAY

During one of our many weekends at the beach, I noticed while I was walking Winn that her right hind leg would occasionally drag. She'd had arthritis in that hind quarter for about six years. We started Winn on Glucosamine a few years earlier at the vet's suggestion, but Winn hated to take pills and would hide under the bed rendering "pill time" a virtual no go. In February of 2006 I took Winn for her annual check up and mentioned how her right leg seemed to "slip," and that giving Winn pills was a huge challenge. He suggested I give her baby aspirin at morning and at night saying a pill as small as that might be easier to hide in some food than larger pills. I started her on that regimen immediately. When we were at the beach, we'd give her a pill before her first morning walk so it would kick in by her "doughnut walk". She was still very enthusiastic about her walks, so I took it as a sign that the aspirin was working.

While I took her for her last walk before bed, she tripped off the curb. I thought her back leg gave out on her, but in reality, Winn didn't see the curb at all. She was mortified. Winn put her head down and wagged the little tip of her tail. I gave her a pat and assured her that no one had seen the incident. We continued on our walk, but I began instituting the words "careful" and "this way" into her vocabulary. For my part, I made sure she used ramps instead of curbs whenever possible and, we stayed in well-lit areas.

One night in April, Winn seemed disoriented. She paced in our bedroom not able to decide whether to lie on her bed or under our bed. Ken and I had seen this behavior before, but typically it was during a thunderstorm. Winn was terrified of thunder and at the first rumble, often hid under our bed and started chewing the frame. After an hour of pacing and chewing, I took her down to the living room trying to get her settled. She walked into the wall and was panting heavily. After another hour of this behavior, I told Ken I was taking her to the vet to have her euthanized. I was certain she was suffering a stroke. I put Winn in the car, and she perked up. She stuck her head out the window and had, what looked to be, a huge smile on her face. I thought to myself, *Oh my gosh! I'm going to have Winn put to sleep and she looks so happy and healthy. What am I doing?*

The hospital technicians met me at the door and asked what was wrong. I tearfully told them that I thought Winn had suffered a stroke and that she needed to be put to sleep. We went right into an examination room and waited for the on-call vet. I looked down at Winn. She had her head between my legs. I could not stop sobbing. I looked in vain for a tissue, which I figured would be a standard supply at a vet E.R. and settled for a wad of paper towels. When the vet came into the room, she looked at me and my wad of paper towels and then looked at Winn, who removed her head from between my legs to see who spoke. I explained that I thought Winn had suffered a stroke and told the vet Winn's symptoms. I also mentioned that Winn had just had a check up two months earlier. Other than the stiffness and soreness from arthritis, she was in perfect health. With that information in mind, the vet decided not to do any blood work. She said she thought Winn had the onset of dementia. Given Winn's advanced age of thirteen and a half this was a common diagnosis. The vet sent us home with a bottle of pills that would help keep her calm during further episodes. I gave her one before we left the clinic thinking it would start to work by the time we got home, but Winn stayed up until six in the morning when the rest of the house was waking up.

TAKE THE GOOD WITH THE BAD

While Winn never had an episode that severe again, there were noticeable changes in her. Not all of them were bad. During the night Winn would sometimes pant very heavily, and in the morning something would be different about her. It was as if her brain got stuck. She'd stand by the couch and bark for reasons only she knew. Some of the changes were sweet. Winn began to interact with us on a regular basis. We'd practically trip over her as she was constantly at our side. She also seemed to relax quite a bit and began to smile in a senile sort of way that endeared us to her even more.

The oddest behavior of all, I think, was when Winn decided to swim. She always seemed to like water; she enjoyed wading in the stream near our house and she sought out puddles after it rained. One day in April, we were at the beach, and the weather was unseasonably warm. Ken and the boys were knee boarding in the bay, and I took the dogs for a walk around the community. We walked by the duck pond on our way back to our house. The ducks were quacking at Winn and Lucky, and Winn took off at a run and jumped into the pond and swam after the ducks. Not to be undone, Lucky followed suit. Winn swam after the ducks, and the ducks flew away after their threatening quacks went unnoticed. Every walk after that, until the weather turned too cold, included a swim in the pond.

When Winn heard a thunderstorm or fireworks, she still paced and worried. Medicine seemed to calm her some, but the best way to get her to relax was to lift her onto the bed and have her lie down at my feet. I don't know why it was my feet. Lucky figured out his place on the bed immediately. He put his head on one of the pillows and lay next to me. I would offer Winn a pillow, but she always refused, preferring to be near the end of the bed next to my legs.

Winn physically slowed down as a result of her heavy panting. She no longer pulled me on the leash. Instead, I started to pull her. I sometimes could only coax her to walk up the hill to our house with the words "Frosty Paw." Those magic words meant a delicious frozen treat made just for dogs, and the mention of one would give Winn the energy to walk the last few yards to our door. Winn slowed down in other ways as well. When the doorbell would ring, Winn no longer bothered to get up and bark unless it was a food delivery person. Winn had become highly motivated by food; she still sounded vicious, but she would stop barking to lick her chops.

By the beginning of September 2006, it became increasingly clear that the aspirin we were giving Winn was not working. Winn seemed very uncomfortable, and I knew I had to call the vet.

WINNSDAY

The school year beginning that September was stressful for all of us. Both Alex and Tim were starting new schools. Alex was staying on the same campus but moved to middle school, while Tim changed schools completely. There was the stress of homework, locker combinations, finding classrooms and making friends. For me, I had the stress of trying to figure out how to get the boys to and from school when they both started and finished at the exact same time, plus trying to help them do homework and figure out what assignments were due each day. Alex found his niche right away, as he knew most of his classmates from his lower school, but Tim had a harder time. He was very quiet and tried to feel out his teachers and classmates.

One day I was at the computer helping Tim with his homework and looked out the window to see Winn panting heavily and looked dazed and confused. When she tried to go to the bathroom, her hips looked as though they could not support her. I called the vet, and they told me to bring Winn in first thing the next morning.

I brought the boys together and told them I thought Winn was going to have to be euthanized when I took her to the vet. They were devastated. Alex was very demonstrative with his emotions. He began to cry and yell. He screamed that I was a murderer. He told me I was giving up on Winn; that I must not have really loved her. It was incredibly hard to hear, but I really admired his ability to open up the flood gates of his emotions. Tim was much quieter, and that actually concerned me more. With the new school year only being two weeks old, he was still pretty stressed out and reserved. With the news about Winn's possible demise, I was afraid he'd withdraw completely. Tim went up to Winn and started petting her and loving her up, and he told her what a good dog she was, and that God would take good care of her. Tim told Winn she'd feel better in heaven. Then he and Alex sat next to her and stroked her fur so softly.

We all cried ourselves to sleep that night. I'm not even sure how much sleep I got. I felt that it was such an awesome and awful responsibility to make the decision to put Winn to sleep. I prayed to God to give me a clear sign that I was doing the right thing. Winn could not get comfortable on her bed. She'd get up and lie back down making a loud groan when she did. I kept asking God *Was that it? Was that the sign that I'm doing the right thing?* Winn got up several times during the night to get a drink of water. I'd ask God *Was that it? Was that the sign that Winn is having kidney failure and I'm doing the right thing?*

The next morning the boys tearfully said goodbye to Winn, and I took them to school. Before I did, though, I emailed their teachers and told them what was happening. That way if the boys seemed quiet or tearful, the teachers would have a heads up. Alex's teacher told me that Alex told her right away. I was so glad that he felt comfortable with his new teacher. Tim's teacher emailed me that she would be there for Tim if he wanted and said that she knew what we were going through as she had to euthanize her beloved thirteen-year-old dog that summer. I felt both boys were going to be all right.

I took Winn to the vet. I left her in the car while I signed her in. I explained that I wanted to keep Winn in the car until her appointment because her hind legs kept giving out on her and I was afraid she'd slip on the linoleum floor. I also was going to try to tell the woman at the front desk that I had made the appointment because I was sure Winn needed to be euthanized, but I couldn't get that last part out because I couldn't hold back the tears any longer.

I know from personal experience that when people are in physical or emotional pain they act out. We cry or shout or become withdrawn or defensive. We blame others or ourselves for our misfortunes. As a professional who deals with this on a daily basis, it is immensely draining to be at the receiving end of anguish. I did not envy the receptionist one bit for being at the receiving end of my tears at nine o'clock in the morning. While I'm sure this woman has been through every scenario associated with every domestic animal, she probably wanted to get to lunch without someone sobbing in her face. I couldn't help myself, and I hope she knows how grateful I am that she was there. She is truly a credit to her profession.

So this compassionate woman followed me out to the car and opened the door and started talking to Winn. Winn looked up and wagged the little tip of her tail. Oh I loved when she did that, and a fresh batch of tears came flooding out. The woman told me that Winn was quite responsive and alert. She explained to me that most animals that the veterinary practice euthanized did not respond at all to other people. They just lay in one spot. She told me she would look for me outside when it was my turn. I thought of giving her a hug, but figured she needed a break from my emotional outbursts. I lifted Winn from her seat and walked her around the grounds of the hospital. She seemed to really enjoy herself. We walked for about twenty minutes and were called inside for our appointment.

The vet came into the room, and I burst into tears. I didn't know I had any tears left, but apparently, I tapped into the reserve supply. She asked me what was going on, and I told her how Winn couldn't walk without slipping, and how her legs would give out. I told her how uncomfortable Winn was and the two baby aspirins didn't seem to help. The doctor examined Winn. She asked me about Winn's appetite and her behavior. I remarked that Winn loved to eat and stuck to us all like Velcro. I even mentioned that I thought Winn's extra weigh might be hurting her hips even more. Then the vet told me something I didn't expect. She told me that she didn't think Winn was ready to go. She said arthritis is not terminal, and that there was medicine—chewable medicine that tasted good—that she thought would help Winn. The vet added that Winn's eating was a good thing. It was keeping her going. Food was something she looked forward to. She didn't see Winn slipping during the appointment, but said there were booties with grippers I could buy to keep her steady on her feet. The vet also said that she knew I came to the appointment thinking Winn was going to have to be put to sleep, and she recognized the mental preparation it took to come to that decision. So the vet asked if I would prefer Winn be euthanized. I didn't even think about it and told her no.

So we left the office with a trial size amount of joint compound and an anti-inflammatory medicine. She gave me a thirty-day supply, and told me I could always get more, or I could bring Winn back if she didn't seem any better or got worse. I put Winn in the car, got the medicine, and checked out. The woman who was so helpful when I checked in said she thought the medicine would be really good for Winn. Again, I cried.

All the way home, I sobbed. I was relieved, but I was also angry at myself for thinking I could make a decision so final without any clear sign that it was necessary. Was I acting on my perceptions? Was I so worried that Winn was already suffering that I wanted to put her to sleep before she got worse? I felt terrible and wonderful at the same time. I felt extremely fortunate to have had such a caring and compassionate and knowledgeable vet.

When Winn and I got home, I emailed the teachers and let them know what happened. Then I called the schools to make sure the teachers read their emails. The secretary at Tim's school was wonderful. I tried to explain that Tim thought Winn was going to be put to sleep, but actually she was very much alive.

The secretary laughed joyously with me and when I said she must think I'm nuts, she told me that my story wasn't the first one she'd heard. She told me it probably happens more that we know. I was overcome by her kind words.

Alex's teachers were thrilled! When his homeroom teacher gave him the news, he couldn't believe it. His classmates rallied around him yelling and giving high fives. His other teacher even offered another diagnosis for Winn. No one in the class had homework that night in honor of *Winnsday*.

After that tumultuous day, Alex and Tim easily settled in to the routines of their schools. They knew they could go to their teachers if they had a problem and their concerns would be validated. I will always be grateful for the love and kindness the teachers showed to all of us that day.

BEDS, GATES, AND WALKS

There was a big celebration in the Carle household that night and the rest of the week was spent "Winn proofing" the house. The first order of business was buying baby gates. Winn was restricted from using the stairs except to get upstairs at night and come down the following morning so we put a gate at the bottom of the first floor stairwell. We also gated the living room from the kitchen and the dining room—I don't think we had this many gates for the boys when they were little. Winn had always eaten her meals upstairs, while Lucky has his in the kitchen. Now, since they'd be on the same floor, having gates separating half the house was necessary to keep mealtime from being fight time.

These gates seemed to be a lot more complicated than what I remembered with the boys. I had to put three pieces of metal together, and the ends needed to be screwed into the walls. What happened to the old fashioned wood and plastic one-piece gates that suction cupped to the wall? These gates were very sturdy, that's for sure.

Next up: the orthopedic bed. We bought a thick egg crate textured bed online and had it shipped overnight. Winn's regular pet store model bed was replaced by a model made specifically for older dogs and dogs with arthritis. We had bought a bed from this company for Dixie, and she loved it. This bed was the new and improved model. When we got it delivered the next day, the boys and Ken and I took turns laying on it. It was extremely comfortable. Tim remarked that he might like this type of dog bed to sleep on. Winn adapted very quickly to her new set up.

The vet told me that Winn had to go on a walk everyday. This was something we did several times a day at the beach. When we were in town, though, I just let her out the back door into our fenced yard. The vet said that the walks would keep her joints limber, and even if we just went up to the end of the street and back, it would do Winn a world of good. Winn was so excited! Her heart was so much more willing than her body.

We started off going up one block, over one block, down two blocks, then home. Winn's hind legs betrayed her and she would slip almost the entire way. After taking the medicine for about two weeks, our walks extended to the next block and she had better control of her hind legs. We didn't go fast. Our walks took about twenty minutes only going eight short blocks. Long gone were the days when Winn pulled and lunged while at the end of her retractable leash.

For the first time in the twelve and a half years that I owned her, we no longer needed the choke chain. It was so great to see Winn comfortable and happy.

IS ANYBODY LISTENING?

By November, it became apparent that Winn was having difficulty hearing us. She'd look at me when she saw me, but did not respond to her favorite words, namely "walkie, walkie" and "Frosty Paws." We quickly developed hand signals for Winn. Patting our legs meant "come here," pointing to her bottom meant for her to "sit." Pointing to the floor meant for her to "lay down." The leash, of course meant it was walkie time. It seemed that her hearing was almost completely gone by the end of the month. She could feel vibrations and knew when I was walking on the floor of the room she was in, and she could hear high pitches like Lucky's mealtime bark and a whistle.

Lucky became the dinner bell for Winn. When Lucky would sing his can opener song, Winn would come into the kitchen and nudge me on the leg to let me know she was ready to eat. In the past, Lucky's high pitched bark could be a source if irritation to us all. Winn would even growl at him to get him to stop. After Winn lost her hearing, the yip became immensely helpful to her.

Winn ignored the doorbell late in her life when she could hear, figuring it was for one of the boys, which it was, but she couldn't hear conversations either, so she would be surprised to find herself gated in the living room while we had guests in the dining room, and she would bark ferociously from her side of the house.

I felt bad for her in some ways. If she was asleep, and we walked by her and patted her on the head, we'd startle her. I guess it really is best to let a sleeping dog lie. On the other hand, her sense of smell, touch and taste were very acute. She was always a sniffer. In fact before I stopped running with her, I often accused Winn of sniffing so she wouldn't have to run any further. I'd call those runs "calorie keepers." But when she lost her hearing, she sniffed everything and everyone. If you put food in the microwave or oven, she'd be in the kitchen in a flash.

Her sense of taste seemed sharpened, too. While she'd always been a polite beggar, she could be very picky about what she'd beg for. No more. If she smelled it, she'd ask for it. If one of us was carrying a plate of food from one room to another, Winn would nudge us in the back of the knee as a reminder that she would appreciate a taste. If by chance we forgot to give her something, she would give us such a sad look, that we were made to feel guilty. In fact, one time Alex felt so badly about not saving her a piece of his bacon, he took his plate out of the dishwasher so she could lick it.

HAVE GATES, WILL TRAVEL

Except for a few odds and ends, everything we need we keep at the beach house. There were a few occasions where the back of our SUV was filled almost to capacity with things to make Eastern Shore living easier, but mostly the trips were stow-and-go. We'd stow the kids and the dogs and every once in a while our hamster or toad and go Downy Ocean as they say in Baltimore. Our first trip after Winn's diagnosis from the vet involved adding gates.

Now, the beach house already had two gates. One was for the steps so Winn could go upstairs and eat in peace. When she was done, she would stand at the top of the stairs and woof to let us know she had finished eating and was ready to come back down. We would pick up Lucky's bowl and pick up Winn's bowl and move the gate. The other gate was out on our deck.

We love having the dogs join us out on the deck. We are out there all the time. We sit at the table and eat lunch or dinner, or sometimes just appetizers while watching boats go up and down the canal. The boys can go crabbing off of our pier. Any caught crabs that are five inches in width or bigger go into the crab pot to be consumed later. Lucky would go nuts knowing that there were crabs scratching against the metal sides trying to get out of the pot. Every once in a while a crab would escape and side step off the dock and back into the water. Before we had the gate, Lucky, who always comes back when he is called, went off the deck in pursuit of a crab and got pinched on the nose, so the gate protected other dogs from Winn and protected Lucky from the crabs.

Then we added another gate. Winn couldn't eat upstairs anymore, so we gated the den for Winn's meals. Winn adapted well and patiently "woofed" each time she wanted to be let out of gated area like the den, or wanted to be let onto a gated area like the deck. The boys were very agile and stepped over the gate in the den to play their video games or jumped over the gate on the stairs. Considering the circumstances leading up to our little gated community, we all adapted nicely and felt very grateful that Winn was still with us.

I BECAME A SEEING EYE HUMAN

Over the months, Winn would pant heavily at night and something would be amiss in the morning. She had developed a Parkinsonian affect that would cause her to get "stuck" in doorways. It was as though Winn was waiting for all the neurons on her brain to function together in order to allow her to take a step. We never urged Winn to hurry up. She moved when her body was ready, and we either walked around her or took a different path.

One day she walked full stride into the back door. When I gave Winn a pat on the head to make sure she was okay, she got startled. She didn't see me standing beside her. She didn't appear to be able to see at all. I managed to get Winn to move to the side in order to open the door for her to go out. She must have remembered the small step from the back door to the portico because she stretched her toes out on one paw and reached out to feel where that step was. She stepped down without falling and walked right into the trashcan. She was dazed and disoriented, but thankfully, not hurt.

I had read years before that animal keepers at the zoo train elephants by touching them on the side that keepers want the animals to go. If the elephant is touched on the left side, for example, the elephant will turn to the left. As it turns out, this worked for Winn as well. Winn did remarkably well remembering where things were on the first floor. We thought she could make out shapes or shadows, but mostly she relied on her memory. She remembered where the chairs and tables were on the first floor. She knew how to get to the back door to be let out. She also would lay on the rug by the front door if she wanted to go for a walk.

Outside of her familiar surroundings, I became her eyes. I spoke to her as though she could still hear, but used the leash to motion to her which way to go on our walks. She would walk by my side, often her shoulder would touch my leg, and that's how Winn knew when to go up or down a curb. Our walks became increasingly slower, but also incredibly enriched.

I always said that the power of observation was lost on me. When I was younger, my grandparents had a curio cabinet. When I would go to their house to visit, my grandmother would always ask me if I noticed the new item in the cabinet. Every visit, Nanny would bring me into the living room, lead me to the curio cabinet and ask "What's new or different in the cabinet, dear?" I was always stumped. I'd guess, and my grandmother would tell me to try again. I'd ask for clues. If my younger cousin was with me, I'd ask her to whisper the answer in my ear. I just never could process details. Years later, I cynically called those curio items "dustables," but I always wished I knew what was new or rearranged without Nanny or one of my cousins telling me.

When Winn and I slowly made our journey around the block or up to the end of our street and back, I had plenty of time to notice things. While Winn sniffed, I looked. I looked up and saw Orion. I didn't know you could see Orion in a Baltimore sky. I had seen the stars making up his belt several times, but the only other time I had seen Orion was in the Caribbean. I also noticed things in my neighbors' yards. Some of my neighbors had the most dazzling displays of chrysanthemums in pots on their front stoops. Other neighbors had the coolest toys for their preschoolers lined up against the sides of their houses.

When December came, I noticed the progressive displays of Christmas lights and decorations going up as Winn and I passed our familiar houses. Some of the decorations were incredibly elaborate. I don't know how or where these people came up with the ideas they had. Other decorations were very simple. A couple of the homes in our neighborhood had candle lights in their windows and a green wreath with a ribbon on their door. I could only imagine how much time and care it took to find the perfect wreath or strand of garland. I knew my neighborhood was pretty, but the year I took my time with Winn, my neighborhood was beautiful. I was thankful to finally notice the details.

When we got our own Christmas tree, I was really nervous about rearranging the furniture. I was afraid Winn would walk into things and hurt herself. She was losing her mind, but she had pride. Winn must have been able to make out the shapes of the furniture in its different spots in the living room. She actually had more space in which to walk. She didn't seem to have any problem manipulating around the tree, either. In fact, she and Lucky enjoyed drinking the water from the tree stand. We didn't put any presents under the tree that year until Christmas Eve night. That was the year we continuously admired our tree and did not have our vision skewed by the gifts under it. Our families also agreed that "this tree was the best tree ever."

Winn and I had our routine down to a science. At night, around 8:00, I'd let Winn outside. While she was out, I'd open up the gate for the stairs and bring her bed up to the bedroom. She'd woof to come in and then walk to the base of the staircase. I'd be upstairs becoming a "Mama in Pajamas" as the boys called me. Winn would woof again, and I'd stand at the top of the stairs, presumably so she could see my shadow. Winn would sway her body back and forth as though coaching her brain and body to work in sync to get her up the steps in an orderly fashion. Sometimes Winn could make her way up the stairs after her woof, other times she had to go to the back door, turn around and try again. She eventually would make it up to her bed. For her reward, I'd pet Winn on the stomach. The medicine she took worked like a charm, but it made patches of skin on her belly dry and itchy. So I became the human loofah. Winn would snort and groan in pleasure. It was the least I could do for her.

In the morning, Winn would get up and stumble around. She would be completely disoriented and find her way into my closet or the bathroom on her way to the staircase. I was on active duty. I didn't let Winn go down the steps on her own anymore. She had missed the bottom step a couple of times before, and I didn't want her to miss more higher up. So, with our privately understood set of hand signals, I'd slowly and gently guide her down the stairs. I'd put my hand on her collar, but I'd let her walk down on her own. I just spotted her. When we got down to the bottom step, I'd walk ahead and try to get the back door unlocked before she walked into it. Unfortunately, 6:00 a.m. wasn't Winn's or my most alert time of the day, so I'd fumble for the key and Winn would walk full stride into the door. So with my series of touches and tugs on her collar, I'd get her out the door, turn on the coffee and bring down her dog bed. Whew, another day began. I always thanked God that Winn made it to another day.

Mealtime also involved coordination. As I worked the can opener, Lucky, who was always a later sleeper, would come down stairs, barge through the closed gate, and begin his can opener song. I'd trip over the dogs as I got their bowls. Winn would become very animated. Sometimes she would join in the chorus, but often, she would stick her head in between my legs at calf level and push her nose against the kitchen cabinet as I put the canned food and canned vegetables into their bowls. Lucky didn't like his dry food and canned food to touch, so he had separate bowls. Winn liked everything mixed together. I'd put Lucky's food down first and then guide Winn to the living room so she could eat hers. Winn had a general idea of where to go. She would eat on the rug in the space between the chairs and the table. This was to prevent her from slipping. I don't know why she chose such tight quarters; maybe she liked knowing there was furniture nearby to catch her if she fell over. Winn would get herself into the living room, but then, I'd have to put her bowl down at nose level, and guide her to her spot. Sometimes we'd have some miscommunication, and she'd go to another part of the living room, so I'd touch her side to get her to turn around, put her bowl down low and try again. I became a valet parker for Winn. I was proficient in dog parallel parking. Winn trained me well.

DEAF BECOMES HER

I often wondered what Winn heard. I knew she could hear high pitches, and unless it was pure coincidence, she looked up when I clapped for her after calling her name. She heard Lucky's yips and knew that it was mealtime, but was there anything else? Was it static in her head or a whooshing sound like the ocean? Was sound distant and far away like a television with almost no volume or nothing at all?

The fact remained that what she didn't hear, didn't bother her. Lucky became head watch dog. He barked at all who walked by our house. He sounded the alarm when the doorbell rang. He ran from the living room window to the dining room window so his soliloquy could still be heard by those that passed. Winn was blissfully unaware. Lucky grew anxious and began eating his fur and scratching himself. He had always had a problem with allergies, for which we had been seeking treatment for a year or so, but his anxiety was provoking his allergies, and his allergies intensified his anxiety. Poor fella. A trip to the doggie dermatologist (there really is such a thing) left us with an arsenal of medicine; some for the morning, some for the night, some for once a week, some for twice a week. We really didn't feel Lucky was living up to his name at that point.

The vet said that Lucky may exhibit some changed behavior while taking his medicines. He had always been a wonderful pill taker and allergy shot receiver. He didn't ever flinch. Every once in a while, though, he seemed to get this errant thought in his head. He would try to jump up on our bed, which had become a no-no years before when he and Winn ate a hole in our mattress, and he would bark for no apparent reason or want to bring us a ball and then not be able to find one and get a bit cranky and confused. Winn was unscathed by any of this. She had no clue her housemate had issues.

One night, Winn was eating out of her food bowl, and Lucky, who was next to me in the computer room, became upset and aggressive. It was clear he wanted her food for himself. I had heard this growl only two times before and both times we had to separate the dogs with either a broom or a blast of water from the hose. It was not a pretty sight. I shoved Lucky's head down near his chest and told him to stop growling. He did not obey. He was intent on showing Winn that he felt threatened by her food eating behavior. Winn still crunched and munched away, completely oblivious to the maelstrom brewing in the next room. After she finished her food, she came into the computer room, as she often did when I was at the computer either writing or reading my emails. Lucky still had his head in his chest and was still growling. Winn came into the room and sat down beside me and put her paw on my leg—she was petting me. I was able to grab Lucky by the collar and take him upstairs until he settled back down. When I came back downstairs Winn resumed her place on the rug next to me and asked for pats while I typed. She never knew that she was the cause of any problem, nor did she seem to care.

GERIATRIC VISIT

Winn had survived another five months since the day I thought we'd have to euthanized her. I made an appointment with the vet who showed us such compassion the previous September. When we arrived at the office, I left Winn in the car and signed her in at the front desk. The woman who didn't send me packing when I burst into tears during the last visit welcomed us back and said she was glad Winn was still with me. I could feel my eyes well up. Geez Louise, not again. I thanked her for the kindness and compassion she showed us the last time we visited, and she said that it was her pleasure. She knew that Winn was blind and deaf and said that this was a geriatric visit. I laughed out loud. At the ripe old age of fourteen and four months, which roughly translated into ninety-eight dog years, I was certain she qualified for such a title. She told me to sit with Winn in the library. I went to the car and gently lifted Winn out of the back seat. I lowered her to the ground and gently tugged her leash. She sat down and didn't budge. I thought she may have been disoriented. I gently pulled her again. If it was possible for her to sit down harder, she did. Finally I lifted her up and carried her into the reception area. From there she walked on her own to the library where she was fed endless tummy yummies by the staff until her turn with the vet arrived.

My left low back was twitching, which I thought was unusual as I didn't have a history of back problems. One visit on the dog scale told me why. Winn was sixty-seven pounds. She gained a whopping thirteen pounds since the vet told us last visit that Winn could eat whatever she wanted as long as it kept her happy. Now Winn was definitely curvy. The vet determined that Winn could still make out shapes and shadows since a little light was going through the clouding of her eyes. She had developed a skin infection that was not in any way related to the medicine shc had been put on. The vet offered to check her blood for geriatric disorders. She thought that Winn's weight gain could be caused by a slowed thyroid. It wasn't. We left with the doctor's orders to cut out snacks. Winn, her belly filled with more tummy yummies the vet gave her, walked on her own out to the car, and sat patiently while I went back in to grab more medicine and pay the bill. I made a follow up appointment for the next month so she could get her rabies shot. It was understood that it would be the one year and not three year inoculation.

SARDS

Lucky got a double ear infection and was absolutely miserable. He shook his head, rubbed it against the wall, and used his paw to scratch the offending site all through the night. I called the doggie dermatologist who offered us an appointment right away. Lucky was given ointment, cleanser and antibiotics to help the poor guy feel better. Within forty-eight hours, Lucky felt almost like his old self. He chased after his ball and wanted the boys to play with him.

A week later, I noticed Winn had an ear infection as well. I called the dermatologist and asked if Lucky's infection was contagious. The vet assured me it was not. I persisted by asking if Winn could take Lucky's medication. (I knew the answer would be "No," but it can't hurt to ask.) The vet did offer Winn an appointment the next day, which I eagerly agreed to take.

Winn not only had a double infection in her left ear, but

she had an infection in her right ear as well. Poor baby. She left with the same medication as Lucky, plus another prescription. Her right ear was so infected, the vet could not see into the ear canal, so he told me to clean her ear with a solution he gave me before inserting the ear drops. We made a follow-up appointment for three week's time.

The solution for Winn's ears splashed everywhere at first, particularly on the right side. After about eight days, I noticed her right eye was shut tight. Winn looked like she was winking. We coincidently had a follow up visit with her primary vet, and I decided to address Winn's eye issue then. The dermatologist was very good about sending his office notes to her primary vet, so she would know what had been happening with Winn's ears.

When we returned to the vet, she had received the faxed report from the dermatologist. She gave Winn a physical, noticed that her thirteen-pound weight gain was holding steady and then examined Winn's ears and eyes. The vet determined that the cleansing solution had splashed into her eye and caused an irritation, which made it painful for Winn to open that one eye. She gave us an ointment for me to rub on her eyelids three times a day, and told me I could just follow up with the dermatologist as scheduled.

While we were in the office, I asked for the vet to check Winn's thyroid again. It had been normal at her last visit, but despite her new Draconian diet, she hadn't lost a single pound. The vet said that Winn absolutely could take medication for a low thyroid. It would certainly not hurt her and would give her an added boost of energy. The medicine was chewable, too.

The eye ointment took about three days to work. Winn could finally open up her right eye. The thyroid medicine seemed to work almost immediately. Winn started jogging in front of me during our walks. When we went to follow up with the dermatologist ten days later, she had lost five pounds! Both Lucky and Winn had their follow-up appointments at the same time. Lucky got a clean bill of health. His ears were essentially normal. Winn's ears looked good, too. I told the dermatologist about Winn's eye and the ointment her other vet had prescribed. I mentioned that Winn's right eye seemed to bulge out now that she could open her eye again. The dermatologist looked alarmed when he saw the condition of Winn's eye and told me to go two doors down to the veterinary ophthalmologist. He told me Winn was suffering from glaucoma. The pressure in her right eye was very high, and he thought Winn must have been in severe pain.

I put Lucky in the truck and felt thankful it was a chilly April day. Winn and I did not have an appointment with the ophthalmologist, so we waited for three hours to see her while the technicians at the dermatologist's office kept periodic tabs on Lucky. When we went into the ophthalmologist's examination room, I felt immediate calm. The staff at this office specialized in older dogs. They whispered and cooed to Winn even though I told them she was deaf. Winn shoved her nose into the technician's knees and wagged her tail. The vet came in and looked at Winn and commented how much pain Winn must be in. I told her that Winn was very stoic; particularly since I had tried to euthanize her twice in the last year because of the pain she had seemed to be in. I meant to think this, but I actually said aloud, "Do you think she'd let me know if she were in pain? It didn't work in her favor in the past."

The vet commented on her deafness and asked if Winn had gained any weight recently. I affirmed that Winn had gained thirteen pounds in five months. The vet asked if Winn slowly went blind or if it happened suddenly. I explained to her that Winn had lost her night vision first, and a few months after that lost all of her sight. The vet diagnosed Winn as having glaucoma, but she also said Winn suffered from SARDS or Sudden Acquired Retinal Degeneration Syndrome.

Dogs who are afflicted with this disorder tend to suffer from deafness, blindness and acute weight gain very rapidly. Many dogs with this condition are euthanized because the owners feel sorry for their pets as the dogs walk into walls and fall off curbs. Veterinarians often recommend euthanasia for SARDS patients because the quality of life for these dogs is so poor. Googling SARDS also pulled up various chat sites in which owners described how depressed their beloved dogs become. The veterinary jury is out as to whether or not dogs can feel the emotion of depression.

Winn, it seemed, had missed her real opportunity to be put to sleep. The ophthalmologist said that euthanasia would not be a good option for Winn because she had adapted very well to her loss of senses. Winn did, however, need to have emergency glaucoma surgery to relieve the enormous amount of pressure that had built up in her right eye. We scheduled the surgery for the following Monday. I wasn't worried so much about the surgery as I was about the anesthesia. I just did not know if Winn would wake up.

When the dogs and I got home, I called a family conference to give everyone an update on Lucky and Winn. Ken and the boys were thrilled at how well Lucky was doing; they also thought surgery was a good idea for Winn since she must be in a lot of pain and not telling us. We prayed mightily that Winn would survive the surgery or that God would give us the strength to handle the devastating loss if Winn did not wake up.

I dropped Winn off for her surgery and asked the office to give me a call to let me know how she was doing. The total time for pre-operative preparations, surgery and recovery would be four hours. It was a bitterly cold April day. The winds were blowing fiercely and trees were tumbling down. I wondered what kind of omen the weather meant. I didn't hear from Winn's surgeon or anyone in the office. I was worried and gave them a call. The heavy winds had caused the ophthalmologist's office to lose power right after Winn's surgery was finished. A tree had fallen on the telephone lines in such a way that the office could not make phone calls, but could receive them. Winn did great and was ready to be picked up at my convenience. The boys and I went to get Winn after stopping to pick up some celebratory Kentucky Fried Chicken. We went in to get Winn and bring her to the truck. As I paid the bill, I looked out the window and saw Alex and Tim taking turns feeding Winn KFC's legendary popcorn chicken. She was sniffing for crumbs and licking the boys' fingers. No one could have guessed Winn had come out of surgery one hour earlier.

NOW

Winn is still hanging in there. She seems comfortable and happy for the most part. Winn has outlived every other dog that was around when we moved to the neighborhood. Some of our neighbors couldn't stand the quiet and within a month brought a new puppy into their house. Others grieved much longer or realized that not having a dog was easier. One family adopted a Hurricane Katrina dog only to realize later that they weren't a true adoptive family, but rather only provided foster care. The true owner came forward, thanks to the chip that the SPCA in Mississippi had installed in the dog. One family was filled with joy; the other was filled with sadness all over again.

Whenever Winn is lying on her bed downstairs and the boys call to me to "come here" I always ask if Winn is still breathing. My fear is that the boys will find Winn has passed away before I do.

I've thought a lot about Winn's eventual passing. I will not just be losing a pet but rather I'll be losing a part of me. I got Winn when I was single. We were two girls on the town. No one associated me as being Ken's wife or Alex and Tim's mom. I was just Jen. There is no other part of my single life left. I have traded everything now. My identity has changed.

I have no regrets. I love my life now. I enjoy our routine as a family. I could not ask for a better husband or kids any more wonderful than the ones I have. I have often described my family as "delicious," and they are. I love to listen to them, help them, and ask them for help. My life is fulfilled knowing that every day I wake up I begin anew with my family.

Sometimes I miss the times when it was just Winn and me. I miss the solitude that went with being single, but I don't miss the loneliness. Some days I long to not have to answer to anybody, but I would miss it more if my children or husband didn't want to engage me in a conversation or a task.

Winn and I needed each other equally, I think. We both got second chances. She got a new lease on life, quite literally, and I learned to love again; first with her, then with Ken and the boys. I have discovered that it is so true that the more you love, the more capable you are to love. Love doesn't run out, a heart can just get bigger and bigger.

When the weather became mild, Alex and Tim and I were walking around the yard looking to see if any bulbs were starting to come up. We found signs of hyacinths, daffodils and tulips. When we came to the back yard Alex discovered that one of our lilac trees is dying. We have three of them planted in a cluster, and for esthetics' sake, I don't think that one of them dying is going to look that bad. Lilacs happen to be my favorite tree, and I love the sweet scent of the flowers. I'll often cut some of the blooms and put them in a vase in the dining room. You can smell the fragrance everywhere on the first floor.

Winn has always enjoyed lying in the shade under the lilac trees. When the wind blows, her back will be covered with tiny lilac petals. I think she feels quite special when this happens, as though she is part of nature's adornment.

Alex and I both decided that when the dying lilac needs to be dug out, we will bury Winn in that spot. It doesn't feel sad to make these plans, but it does seem right. Tim is already working on the guest list for who should attend our funeral service.

For the moment, we just enjoy Winn. We feel relief when we see that she is still breathing in the morning. We feel comfort knowing that she loves being around us for food and for pats. We all feel truly blessed for having Winn in our lives.

EPILOGUE

On August 8, 2007, Winn had a check up with her vet. Everything was fine, and I got refills on her medication and checked out. Winn and I swung by the house, picked up Lucky, and headed to the beach. Both dogs had a wonderful time swimming in the pond, taking walks, and eating goose poop. Winn earned the name "Moochie Poochie" because she always managed to find her way out to the deck to ask for a taste of whatever I was eating at the time.

When we came home on August 19, both dogs were tired and went to their beds. The next morning Lucky was revived, but Winn chose to sleep instead of eat or go for a walk. I cooked beef livers, ground lamb and brown rice thinking homemade dog food would stimulate her appetite. She ate tiny morsels, but nothing more. Winn began to pant very heavily whenever she got up to get a drink.

On Sunday, August 26, Ken and I both came to the conclusion that Winn was ready to leave us. I called the vet and made an appointment for her to be euthanized later that morning. I told the boys to spend some time with Winn saying goodbye. It was surreal knowing that we only had three hours left with her.

Ken and a neighbor lifted Winn and her dog bed into the back of our SUV. I drove slowly and carefully, and prayed that I got every red light. When I parked at the vet hospital, I left Winn in the car. I checked her in, but would not bring myself to write in my "reason for visit." I asked if I could wait outside with Winn, and the staff told me they would come get us when it was time for our appointment. I had to sign a document saying that I gave my permission for Winn to be euthanized. Seeing the description of her visit in print sent streams of tears down my cheeks. I asked if Winn could be carried into the room while remaining on her bed. The staff said they would wheel out a table, lift her and her bed onto it and wheel her into her room.

Winn was wheeled into her room, and we waited. She didn't move except to lift her head when the vet touched her. He gave her an injection of anesthesia and said she would fall into a deep sleep within four to five minutes. I sat in a chair next to her table and rubbed her side as her body twitched into a sedative state. I felt compelled to look at my watch. I guess I wanted to see how many minutes I had left with Winn. The vet came back into the room three minutes after giving Winn the injection and said he was going to give her the injection of barbiturates that would stop her heart. He told me that the second injection would work in less than one minute. I stood over Winn and gently touched her face.

The vet then informed me that Winn "passed on." I asked if he was sure, and the vet nodded his head and told me to take as much time as I needed with her. I stood over her, petting her still warm body until I forced myself away. I took off her collar and went to the reception area to check out. I started shaking and felt tears run down my face. I didn't want to let go of her collar long enough to wipe my face on my t-shirt. The staff told me when I could pick up Winn's remains and assured me that I did not have to pay for Winn's appointment at that time.

I got into my car and prayed to God to give me the strength to drive home safely. I also asked God to give me a sign that Winn made it to heaven. I got home and greeted the boys and went to bed. I couldn't keep my eyes open, but I couldn't sleep either. We all went out to the mall and to a show as a diversion. I bought a CD, and Ken asked me if I wanted to put my purchase in the car. I initially said that I could hold on to it, but then I changed my mind and decided to put the CD in the car. My eyes were pulled upward to the sky. Right above me was a dark gray cloud in the shape of Winn's head. The cloud had a piece missing where her eye would be and cloud wisps coming out, which looked like a tongue. I knew at that moment that Winn made it to heaven. I had goose bumps on my heart.

Goodbye, sweet puppy. Thank you for the memories.